FINDERS
KEEPERS

OTHER BOOKS
BY JASON PEACOCK

The New Guy

Knuckle Sandwich

Red Carpet Workshop Participant Guide

FINDERS KEEPERS

HOW TO FIND AND KEEP
THE CUSTOMERS YOU WANT

JASON P PEACOCK

BOOKLOGIX®

Alpharetta, GA

ISBN: 978-1-63183-751-7 - Paperback
eISBN: 978-1-63183-752-4 - ePub
eISBN: 978-1-63183-753-1 - mobi

Library of Congress Control Number: 2020902970

Printed in the United States of America   0 2 1 4 2 0

♾ This paper meets the requirements of ANSI/NISO Z39.48-1992 (Permanence of Paper)

Doyle Johnson was my personal haberdasher. More importantly, he was my friend.

When it came to customer care, Doyle personified the very principles I've tried to convey in this book. I can think of no better person to dedicate this to.

He always made me feel like a million bucks. Anytime I was out for a night on the town, I would take a selfie in my Doyle Johnson threads and send him a pic. He would always respond with, "Looking good, my man."

I actually felt taller, leaner, and more professional while wearing a Doyle-made suit. Could I have found clothing for a cheaper price? Of course! But they wouldn't have had his signature peacock blue suit liners or my name stitched on the inside pocket. He focused on providing the little details that make all the difference—and it was appreciated.

Doyle, you are missed, my friend. I hope this book will shed some light on the principles you lived every day.

CONTENTS

Part 5: When?

ACKNOWLEDGMENTS

To the Fab Five—Wendy, Tanner, Cameron, Kylee, and Sammy—thank you for your continued support and encouragement.

To the queen of keeping customers, Tricia Hushmire—thank you for being a great teammate all these years.

To Big John—from coast to coast, we have certainly covered some ground over the years. Thank you for being the ultimate road-trip partner and an even better friend.

To Don and Cole at Smitty's—a writer's desk is usually a lonely place. Thank you for letting me post up and smoke stogies while writing this. The cold beverages didn't hurt either.

To the crew at BookLogix—thank you for giving aspiring writers like me a platform to share their stories.

And finally, to the sales professionals who dot the fruited plain—thank you for putting yourselves out there every day. In our profession, we face rejection and frustration on a daily basis. Keep your chin up and keep hammering. If this book helps you find or keep at least one customer, then it was worth every minute it took to write it!

INTRODUCTION

December 2014. I was standing in the checkout line with a shopping cart full of gifts. Fellow shoppers had their game faces on, ready to pounce on the next open register. Before I could nudge my way past the old lady in the scooter, my phone rang. I looked at the screen, saw it was my office number, and my heart sank. My longtime account executive, Tricia Hushmire, broke the silence with, "Well, it's over."

"It" was our long-term relationship with a client—the client that just so happened to be the largest client in our agency. The client that represented well over six figures in annual commissions for us. The client that, just a few months earlier, gave us a raving review on our annual customer survey.

As I began to take items *out* of my cart, my mind raced. How could this happen? We were the only nonemployees who got invited to their company Christmas party every year. They never even talked with other agents, much less moved their business to one. What changed?

No sooner had I asked myself that question did the answer appear: *we* did.

I hated to admit it, but we had grown to take them for granted. We had become the very thing we once hated about other agencies. They focus on the product, not the people. Clients become a number, not a person. We had become so focused on their policies, we neglected our own policy.

When we started our agency in 2002, I often used the slogan "More than a policy." In the early days, if I said it once, I said it a hundred times: "When you buy from us, you get far more than an insurance policy. You get me, my team, our experience, and our undivided attention." We built our agency on those principles.

There I was, twelve years later, "successful" by all industry standards, but feeling like a failure. I had failed my client. I didn't jump on an issue like I should have when it first arose. That issue, combined with some others, had grown into something monumental that resulted in our firing. Even more embarrassing was that I had failed to *live* the very words I wrote in a previous book: "The best time to kill a monster is when he's little."

Those words repeated in my head like a broken record. I wrote that s%@#! I must say, it's very humbling to eat the words you write. In case you are wondering, they taste like, well, you know.

Anytime we lose, we have the decision to either become bitter or better. I choose better. Upon losing such a large amount of income, many would reach for a bottle. My thought was, "Why not write a book?" If you can't use your losses to help other people win, what good are they? So, in the words of Ron Burgundy, "You're welcome."

Enough with my personal therapy session—let's get on with it. In the following pages, we're going to dig deep into the five questions that, when asked consistently, will help you find and keep the customers you want. These questions were best asked by Vinnie Barbarino in the 1970s TV series *Welcome Back, Kotter*. It seemed anytime Vinnie was called upon in class, he instantly turned the tables on Mr. Kotter by peppering him with his own questions. They were simply who, where, what, how, and when. In reality, Vinnie was just creating a diversion so that he and his fellow Sweathogs could get back to their tomfoolery. We are going to ask these questions not to create a diversion, but to help us create a plan.

Before we begin, I do need to give this disclaimer: the principles in this book are exactly like dental floss. I recently asked my dentist which teeth I needed to floss. He said, "Only the ones you want to keep!"

The same is true of building a customer base. Only apply these principles and practices with the customers you *want* to keep. As you will soon learn, there are some you need to lose (customers—not teeth).

So, if your pay is based upon finding new customers or keeping the ones you have, you need to read this book. If it's not, then put it down and go back to watching Netflix. Either way, I appreciate you buying it.

PART 1
WHO?

CHAPTER 1

MATCHMAKER

I can't imagine being single. I thank God every day that my wife, Wendy, said yes over twenty-five years ago. I'm not sure if I could have competed in the dating world of today. I learned everything I knew about attracting the ladies from watching the smooth moves of Larry from *Three's Company*. He roamed the inner sanctum of the Regal Beagle like a lion stalking his prey, his shirt unbuttoned just enough to lay out the welcome mat of chest hair, his gold medallion nestling nicely in said chest hair, and his pants always slightly on the tight side—but not too tight to prohibit him from engaging in a sultry dance of disco.

Yeah, I think I would be in trouble today.

Back in the old days, you had to verbally ask someone out for a date. Can you imagine the hassle of that? Actually having to talk to someone? Today, all you have to be is tech savvy. Whether it's Match.com, Singles.com, or my personal favorite, Farmersonly.com, the opportunities are endless. I admit, I actually laughed while typing that last one. You have to give them credit—they are definitely niche players! While finding a potential mate online seems outlandish to me, the results speak for themselves. According to a 2017 study conducted by Stanford, 39 percent of couples met their partner online.

I have a theory as to why. Online dating sites require users to examine and describe *who* they are and *who* they are looking for. As opposed to Larry of *Three's Company*, who simply looked for someone willing to make a bad decision, the online dater of today wants to make a real connection. By describing themselves and the qualities they are looking for in another, the sites then go to work to match them with someone compatible. As the survey above indicates, it's working.

Users of online dating spend time defining who they are and who their ideal match is. I encourage you to do the same exercise with your customers. Ask yourself, who are your best customers? If you could clone a specific customer and have your entire portfolio resemble them, who would it be?

The reason I encourage you to clearly identify *who* you want as a customer is because that is exactly what I was forced to do in 2015. Still reeling from the Christmas firing, I embarked the new year with as much optimism as I could muster. It didn't take long for that optimism to be tested. In the first quarter, I lost four of my top five clients! Read that again.

Now, I know what you're asking: "Why did I buy this book again?" Stay with me—it gets better.

My entire career, I had prided myself on client retention. I NEVER lost an account. I was the guy who went a solid decade without losing a single client. Now, in the course of three months, I had lost four clients that made up a large portion of my annual income.

My first thought was to throw on a vest and become a greeter. Unfortunately, they weren't hiring. Seeing as though my living expenses didn't seem to care about my recent misfortune, I had to make up the lost income and replace those customers. But with whom?

I am embarrassed to say that up until that point, I had never truly examined the characteristics of my customers. I was so busy working *in* my business that I didn't work *on* my business.

CHAPTER 2

PROBLEM CHILD

In addition to noticing the size of my commission check shrinking, I noticed something else. My phone wasn't ringing nearly as much. In fact, it wasn't ringing at all. I would go days without a single call from a client. No emails, no texts, no voicemails. Crickets.

After a week or so of silence, I realized something. While the four exiting clients made up roughly 40 percent of my income, they accounted for almost 100 percent of my problems. Did you see that?! Virtually all of my day-to-day hassles and stress came from the servicing of those four clients.

While they paid me a large chunk of money, the demands they placed on me and my team had grown to a level we simply couldn't meet. Phone calls and texts at all hours of the day. Requests for things that we shouldn't—and couldn't—do. I dreaded talking to them. It was always something, and no matter what we did, it never seemed to satisfy them. I laughed at jokes that weren't funny, bought meals for people I didn't even like, and spent countless hours on problems I should have never attempted to solve. I felt like I was walking on eggshells 24-7. Not fun.

As you can see, it took me several years to come to grips with the truth of this next statement:

The customer *isn't* always right.

Like me, I'm sure that you have been taught the opposite. But think through the customers who are your proverbial problem children. I guarantee you that one of the issues you constantly face with them is the "fact" that they know everything. They are God's gift to business and have been there and done that more times than you ever will. Just ask them—they will be more than happy to tell you about their accomplishments.

The best thing that could ever happen with these

customers is for them to become someone else's problem. I know, you bought this book to improve your customer-keeping skills, not customer-losing skills, but hear me out. If your goal is to increase your business while enjoying the process, the sooner you say adios to Mr. Know-It-All, the better. They are the ones who will put you in compromising positions, because they always get their way. They are bullies. Always have been, always will be. Life is too short to subject yourself to that.

Remember, you can't make a good deal with a bad guy.

CHAPTER 3

ALL YOU CAN EAT

When my daily emergencies vanished, I suddenly had time to think. In this newfound spare time, I got to work on my *who* strategy, defining who I actually wanted to work with going forward. To help me, I enlisted the services of my advisory board: my wife, Wendy, and my two account executives, Tricia and Amanda. We went through my customer list looking for the traits that our favorite customers had in common. We asked questions like:

- Regardless of the size of the account, were they someone we would want to continue servicing?
- Are they high maintenance?
- Do they let us do our job, or do they tell us how to do it?
- When we see their name on the caller ID, what is our response?

This exercise requires absolute honesty. You have to look past the revenue the customer produces and face reality. If you wouldn't want to replicate them, then why spend another minute trying to keep them? I'm not advocating running off your customers, but if you have any say in your customer portfolio, why not be the one who determines it?

Some of you reading this may be required to service a group of customers you had no hand in creating. That's okay. You can still incorporate the *who* strategies we are discussing. Hang in here with me; I am going to help you create a new and improved clientele.

Over time, you will notice that you gravitate toward some of your customers and shy away from others. That's a good thing. That means you actually care. If you didn't care about servicing customers, you would treat all of them equally—equally bad. Here's why: all customers are NOT created equal.

I don't claim to understand this principle, but everything in me knows it's true. We subconsciously move toward what we want more of, and conversely, we move away from what we want less of. Case in point: my diet. Have you ever eaten just one chip? How about a slice of pizza? Now, for those of us who struggle to eat clean, how many apples do you eat in one sitting? Exactly. You eat one. (While we are on the subject of clean eating, I have a tip for you when it comes to kale. If you add a little coconut oil, it makes it much easier to scrape into the trash! And you were worried about getting some useful information from this book.)

How we choose clientele is kind of like how we fill our plates at an all-you-can-eat buffet. We look at the spread of healthy options and often feel ashamed. We know we should pile our plates with salad and fruit. Instead, we end up seeing how many different pizzas we can sample. Why? Because we know we will eat it! I have never seen a person who's in shape eat at a buffet. Well, that's not entirely true. Round is a shape.

My point? Like attracts like, and the same is true of our business. Your ability to show up every day and engage with your customers at the highest level will only be attainable if you are dealing with people you like. If you genuinely dislike someone, it is impossible to serve them well on a long-term basis. You can fake it for a little while, but eventually you will turn a deaf ear to them. Your service will be subpar, and your current customer will become a former customer.

This isn't to say that your customer roster should resemble a fraternity party. Let me be clear: you will have some customers that you would never have over for dinner. That's okay. We all do. They pay all your invoices on time, they don't complain, and they have bought from you for years. Do NOT send them packing just because they don't give you a high five at the end of a meeting.

What I am proposing is that your customer care and client retention will dramatically improve when your roster resembles that which you move toward. It's pizza versus salad. I promise you, pizza wins. Every time. I have yet to see a salad delivery driver.

CHAPTER 4

SWIPE RIGHT

By now, you have hopefully bought into the idea that there is such a thing as the ideal customer—your *who*—and once found, your highest effort should be in retaining the ones you have and adding as many new ones as possible.

But how do you know who your *who* is? Here are a few things to look for. You want a *who* that:

- Likes you just the way you are
- Allows you to be human
- Appreciates the little things
- Will tell their friends about you
- Is nice to the waiter
- Knows that you are honest (and doesn't have to "keep" you that way)
- Orders the lunch-sized portion
- Sends you a Christmas card

- Asks about your family
- Celebrates your successes
- Is genuinely happy for you
- Treats your staff with respect
- Stays away from "gray areas" that push your boundaries
- Offers to pick up the tab at lunch
- Asks questions, but isn't questioning

Okay, now that you know who you are looking for, the next question is, where can you find them? I'm so glad you asked.

PART 2
WHERE?

CHAPTER  5

LOCATION, LOCATION, LOCATION

Now that you have identified the type of customer you want to work with, where can you find more of them? Wouldn't it be great if we could just "swipe right" for our next customer?

I have spent countless hours and a small fortune over the years searching for the answer to the above question (not the swipe right question—the one right before it). I have hired all types of lead-generation services, I have bought lead lists, I have paid telemarketing companies to make calls *for* me.

The one thing all of the above have in common is this: none of them worked. At least, not for me.

Maybe you are having great success with any or all of the above to keep your pipeline of prospects full. If that's the case, feel free to skip over this section. Although, I'm guessing you wouldn't have bought a book about finding the right customers if we weren't in the same boat.

That being the case, let's figure this thing out together.

To determine the *where*, we need to engage in a similar exercise as we did to discover our *who*. And just like the question of *who*, this process requires absolute honesty. If you can't be honest with yourself about where you originally found your customers—or, in some cases, where they found you—you will not be able to repeat it. I will admit, this examination can be humbling. But what's more humbling is having a dry prospect pipeline.

So, hat in hand, let's get real. Is that cool with you?

Okay, I'll go first.

On the following page is a list of the various *wheres* that created some of my customers. Along with the backstory of each acquisition, I've included the average annual commission dollars these customers bring in to my agency. Because, after all, "If it don't make dollars, it don't make sense!"

WHERE	ANNUAL COMMISSION
Random Call-In	$40,000
Convention Swimming Pool	$80,000
CPA Referral	$150,000
Newsletter Campaign	$120,000
Cold Call	$100,000
Referral from Underwriter	$30,000

The random call-in happened in 1999. It was a brand-new company and they needed insurance. I was the new guy at our office and handled all the call-in business. A day or two later, they walked into my office with the most detailed business plan I had ever seen, along with their checkbook. We put together a proposal, they signed the paperwork, and twenty years later they are still a client of mine—and a very good one, I might add.

The swimming-pool client is one of my favorite stories. We insurance folks like to have a good time (we have to, for our sanity). One of the best times of the year is our annual agents convention. It's a party—a fantastic party! While hanging out in the pool, a fellow attendee asked if I still insured cell-tower contractors. After confirming I did, he informed me his wife served on the same school board as the CFO for one of the top companies in the industry.

Fast-forward three years. I got a call from his wife, who by this time had become great friends with me and my wife. She asked if I would be interested in handling the insurance for a new company she and the aforementioned CFO were starting. Um, yeah! I was interested. We brought them on as a client and serviced their insurance until they sold the company. The good news: they sold to one of our other clients.

The CPA referral client came to us by way of a CPA referral (just seeing if you are paying attention). A friend of ours, who happened to be the CPA for a growing company in our area, called and asked if we would take a meeting with them as a favor. We did. After some discussion, we uncovered that the growing company's agency was charging them exorbitant fees. We offered our suite of services, which were better, at a discounted rate. We secured the order, and over the next several years, this growing company became one of our largest clients.

The newsletter campaign customer is a prime example of simple persistence. I had been sending this particular company various articles of interest and insurance-related correspondence for over five years. For five years, I had never been able to make contact with them. Voicemails went unreturned, and I assumed my written correspondence had all ended up in the same file—File 13, a.k.a. the trash can. That was, until I received a phone call from their controller, who told me he had been receiving my correspondence all these years. He asked if I would be willing to put together some pricing for their upcoming renewal. He informed me I had two weeks to get it done and asked if we could meet that type of deadline. My response? Absolutely! Of course, I didn't tell him we typically need ninety days or more to put together a deal that size.

We rallied the troops, worked all weekend, and enlisted the help of our CEO, who called in a favor with one of our top trading partners and had our proposal ready to deliver in under a week. They became our largest client and went on to refer us into another $100,000 commission account—all from a simple newsletter!

The cold-call example is one in which I take particular pride. I had called this poultry-processing company countless times and I was stuck in "voice jail." One day, I decided to switch up my strategy and try calling after hours. You cold-calling cowboys may want to try a similar strategy, because to my surprise, the CFO I had been trying to reach actually answered his own phone. He was straight and to the point, *and* he had a British accent, which always makes you sound smarter and more intimidating. I started my normal pitch and he stopped me in my tracks.

"Jason, I'm with Marsh, the largest insurance broker in the world," he said. "Why should I take a meeting with you?"

"Mr. Prospect," I responded, "you are correct. Marsh is the biggest broker in the world. But on an account your size, you are getting their C-team. Their A-team is busy calling on Coca-Cola and Home Depot—not your company. With us, you get our A-team. I will be bringing in my partner, Gerald, who grew up on a poultry farm and insures more poultry-related companies than any agent in the country. Is that a good enough reason to take a meeting with us?"

To this day, I don't know how I came up with that response, but he took the meeting. Fast-forward twenty years, and they now account for over $100,000 of revenue per year.

The underwriter referral story brings a smile to my face. When I started in the insurance business back in 1998, one of my mentors, Harold Smith, gave me the following advice: "Jason, you need to spend as much time building relationships with your underwriters and carrier reps as you do your clients."

Harold was a legend in our business. To this day, I model the way I do business after him. He knew the importance of building relationships with trading partners. So, I did. One of those relationships was with a young wholesale broker. We played golf. We met up for happy hour. My submissions went to the top of his stack. He took care of me and my clients. I returned the favor by giving him first shot at the deals on my desk. He called me one day and said, "Jason, I just got screwed by one of my agents. I worked my tail off on a deal for him and he took my proposal and gave it to a competitor. So, next year, if you want to go after that account, I would love to insure it for you!"

Next year, guess what happened? Yep, I went after that account and placed it with my wholesale buddy. I still insure them fifteen years later!

The point of me telling the above stories is to show you that *where* you get your customers doesn't matter. It can be all over the board. What does matter is knowing the origin of your customer base so you can replicate them.

CHAPTER  6

GAME PLAN

Hopefully my *where* examples have gotten your juices flowing. But before you go jumping into a convention swimming pool, let's spend some time pairing our *where* with a strategy on *how* to get the most out of these acquisition sources.

Let's start with the random call-in. Maybe you are the new guy in the office and have the responsibility of responding to call-in business. The biggest challenge in this role is keeping your attitude positive. The reality is that most call-ins will be a complete waste of your time and won't amount to much. However, you never know what may be on the other end of the phone or email.

To be effective in landing quality call-in business, you need to take on the slogan of Planet Fitness. Their mantra is that their gyms are a judgment-free zone. As hard as it may be, you must take on a similar commitment. I once had a call-in prospect — actually, in this case it was a walk-in prospect — fall asleep in my office. He fell into such a deep slumber he actually wet his pants. True story. What did I do? I fumigated my office and threw out the soiled chair. What I *didn't* do was give up on call-ins. It's a good thing I didn't. Later that year, I got the call-in I mentioned in the previous chapter. They became a client and still are, twenty years later.

On to the swimming pool example. The strategy to employ for casual conversations is to be prepared. You have to be ready at all times. You never know where a conversation may lead, which is why casual conversations require preparation. I know that sounds like an oxymoron, but hear me out. When I was asked about my niche, I had an answer, one I had rehearsed many times. I didn't give an aw-shucks response that many in my business offer. I didn't downplay it or apologize for my expertise. I wasn't arrogant with my answer, but didn't mince words either. I knew I could help and made the same offer Delta famously coined: "We are ready when you are." A few years later, they were ready. So were we.

To obtain high-level referrals like the CPA referral mentioned above, the best advice I can give you is to ask for them—often. But when asking, be specific!

Specific questions get specific answers.

Here is what I mean. Countless times, I've heard salespeople ask clients or centers of influence (COIs) if they "know anybody" who could use their services. This question is normally answered with, "Let me think about it and get back to you." Ninety percent of those who ask that question are still waiting for someone to get back to them. Newsflash: it ain't happening.

I will admit, I asked the same question for years, and my referral business was lackluster at best. Here's what I do now.

When I meet with clients or COIs, I have a prepared list of prospects I am targeting. I usually limit it to just a couple of names so I don't firehose them with my ask. I then simply hand them the list, ask if they are familiar with the names, and, if so, what I need to do to get in front of them. In most cases, if they don't recognize the target companies, they will provide a name or two of similar companies. The exchange goes something like this: "Jason, I don't know ABC Construction, but you need to call John Doe at XYZ. XYZ is in that same space and John is a friend of mine."

Done and done.

For the newsletter effort, I have always taken the position that providing value on a consistent basis produces results. Whether it's an email campaign or snail mail, I strive to educate my prospective clients on issues that matter to them. The key is that the content has to be of interest to *them*—not me. If it doesn't add value to their business, I have actually done them a disservice by sending irrelevant information. They will immediately discard it or delete it and probably place my name into their spam filter.

This is where industry-specific articles and tips come in. It shows you know their business. I make it a practice to read the trade magazines and online newsletters of my niche on a weekly basis. I actually built that into my schedule so it doesn't fall prey to my chronic CRS (Can't Remember Sh—Stuff). My goal: for them to view me as a resource that betters their business. I love what my colleague John McGarvey says to prospective clients: "We want to help make you a better business, whether or not we become your broker." With that mindset, you move from a peddler to an advisor. Advisors get paid. Peddlers wind up in voice jail.

Cold-calling is near and dear to my heart. I was introduced to the world of smiling and dialing by a legend in magazine sales, Kent Shannon. Kent owned a company in the Chicago area that sold magazine subscriptions over the phone. He was also the father of one of my best friends, Shane. He hired both Shane and me while we were attending community college and put us to work. I will forever be indebted to Kent for giving me a job. It was while hammering calls in a cubicle that I learned the key to effective cold-calling.

That key: make it a game.

Cold-calling truly is a numbers game, so play it. I would set beat-yesterday goals such as number of dials, number of laughs from customers, number of f-bombs hurled my way, number of hang-ups, etc. All of that led to an increase in the only number that really mattered: number of sales.

As of this writing, I am forty-seven years old. I have been in the sales game for well over twenty years. I still set beat-yesterday goals for my cold-calling efforts. Just yesterday I made sixty dials, talked to eight prospects, and unfortunately didn't have any f-bombs thrown my way. Maybe tomorrow.

The last example of my *where* was a referral from an underwriter. For your purposes, you can substitute underwriter with vendor or supplier. How well do you know your vendors and suppliers? More importantly, how well do they know *you*?

My rule for relationships with suppliers and vendors is simply to never burn a bridge. If you stick around an industry long enough, you will end up running into the same people over and over. While their business cards and titles may change, your relationships shouldn't.

Relationships don't happen by accident. You have to invest in them. One of the ways I have invested in these relationships is through golf. For years, I set aside Friday afternoons for my underwriters and company reps. These Friday outings formed the foundation for my closest business relationships. I can't count the number of deals I have secured while on the links. If golf isn't your thing, find something that is. I have a buddy of mine who takes his vendors and suppliers fishing. Captain Mike, as I call him, owns a very successful agency in southwest Florida—*very* successful. While on his boat, which is worth more than my house, he told me he has paid for the boat many times over by using it for business.

Whether it's golf, fishing, community service boards, church, bridge club, trade shows, conventions, or email campaigns, the *where* doesn't matter. What does matter is how often you are there.

Consistency is the key. Get out of your office and have some fun! Trust me, it works.

CHAPTER 7

THE PIED PIPER

Question: How well do you know your customer's business?

Better question: How well do you know the business your customer is in?

My career took a massive leap forward when I committed to not only getting to know my customers' individual businesses, but also to knowing as much as I could about the businesses they were in: their industry ecosystems. I have made it a study. A constant one.

Every week, I read the industry journals that cover their industry. I attend and often exhibit at their industry trade shows and conventions. I have gotten to know as many people as I can who *also* sell to their industry.

Why?

Because the more people I get to know, the more people get to know me. As I briefly mentioned earlier, I call these folks centers of influence, or COIs. Regardless of their product or service, if we are at the same function or industry gathering, I can guarantee you we are both there for the same reason. That reason is to visit with current clients and build relationships with prospective ones. No one goes to a business networking outing or industry function for the fun of it. We are all there to build our business.

My brother Justin, a highly successful owner of a boutique investment firm, once told me, "Jay, don't ever hesitate walking up to someone at a networking function. They are there for the exact same reason you are. If they weren't, you would both be home sitting on the couch." Thanks, Jut. Great advice!

John McGarvey, my partner in crime and perpetual road-trip partner, has mastered the art of working a room. It doesn't hurt that he's six foot five and a former SEC offensive lineman. He is always the biggest guy in the room. He can simply stand by the bar at cocktail hour and get more business cards than most people working a trade-show floor.

A few years ago, while schmoozing at an industry function, we spotted a guy holding court with several of the key trade-group leaders. He was sort of a Pied Piper. He seemed to know everybody, and, more importantly, everybody knew him. After watching this, I told John, "That's the guy you have to get to know. Win him over, and he can open more doors for you than you can open for yourself." And that's exactly what he did.

Since then, they've become more than just business acquaintances—they're close friends. And the Pied Piper is by far John's most influential COI. To date, he has referred him into several key accounts, including his own company. His endorsement carries huge weight in his industry, and he has helped John get into doors that would otherwise have taken years to open, all in a span of less than three years.

So, who are the Pied Pipers in your ideal customer's industry? Go to the next industry function your customer attends. Then, just stand back and watch.

The Pied Piper will be the person who shakes the most hands and gives out the most hugs. That's the person you need to know—not the one standing in the corner looking at their watch. They're simply passing time, and as soon as their drink tickets are gone, so are they.

Last but not least, to truly become a master networker, you must understand one key principle: those who give more, receive more.

Back to my brother Justin. He goes into every networking breakfast, lunch, or event with a single goal: to *give* at least one referral. By changing your focus to giving instead of receiving, you will become a COI. In the process, you will find yourself on the receiving end of just as many, if not more, referrals for your business.

It's the principle of reciprocity. The next time you walk into a restaurant, open the door for the people behind you and see what happens. One of them will immediately open the next door and usually say something like, "Right back at ya."

See what I mean?

CHAPTER 8

History 101

In finishing up our discussion of *where*, I want you to do one simple task. Pull out your customer list and look at the ones identified as someone you would like more of. Now, simply list where you were when you first met them.

If you want to replicate them, then you have to replicate where you got them in the first place. This is where a lot of folks get into trouble. We tend to write a revisionist history when it comes to recording the events that led to us landing our ideal customer. Two things happen when we roll back the tapes:

1. We have simply forgotten how we got them in the first place. This is especially true when it comes to long-term clients.

2. The situation (or *where*) that led to the sale is no longer cool—or so we think.

Let's talk about the first one for a minute. I am a huge proponent of note-taking. I actually kept daily activity logs for the first five years of my career. I still have them. They are printed out in large three-ring binders. They have survived countless home remodels, raising three children, three different dogs, and a constant parade of my kids' friends. To the untrained eye, they are simple printouts with dates, names, and numbers. To me, they are a reminder of my humble beginnings.

Every call I made, whether it turned out good, bad, or ugly, I documented. Every sale I made, big or small, I documented. Why? Because it's so easy to forget the past. Inside those binders are the keys to the next customer I will land. How do I know that? Because for over twenty years, they have done just that. Simply calling Prospect A led to them becoming a prospective client. Following up that call with subsequent calls and meetings turned that prospect into a paying customer. If it worked in 1999, then the same process will work today for Prospect B. I will grant you that with email, voicemail, caller ID, spam filters, and more, the average prospect is harder to contact. But the fact remains that people still buy from people. Always have, always will.

So, go back to your customer. Where did you meet them? At one point in time, they were a stranger to you. Maybe they called in from an ad. Maybe you met at an industry function. Maybe it was a trade show, a ball game, a networking function. Maybe they were a referral from a friend, classmate, fraternity brother, banker, lawyer, or Indian chief. Here's the thing about where and how you met them—nobody cares!

I wrote about this in my first book, *The New Guy*. As a refresher, so long as the methods you use are ethical and within your company guidelines, nobody cares how you land a client. Your commission statement doesn't discriminate. Why should you?

That leads us to number two. For some reason, we selling brethren often turn up our noses at such outdated methods as cold-calling. We puff up our chests when we land a client via referral, but are almost embarrassed to admit when we win an account the old-fashioned way. Some of the largest accounts I have been fortunate enough to win started with a simple phone call. I didn't know anyone at the company other than the name on a list or website. I didn't have an "in." I had no political clout and certainly wasn't privy to any inside information. I started the process at ground zero. I competed and won.

I have heard well-meaning colleagues brag that they haven't made a cold call in decades. Decades?! If you are so successful and so networked that you already know all the people you need to know, then I have one word for you: bullsh—I mean—congratulations!

I have worked alongside some of the biggest producers in the insurance business and have won a fair amount of business myself. I can tell you without any hesitation, the best are constantly developing new relationships. If it helps, call it "business development" instead of cold-calling. You are paid to be effective, not original! It's kind of like admitting you actually *like* Nickelback. Nobody admits it, and yet, anytime I hear one of their songs, everyone is singing along. And, somehow, they know every word.

In short, if it worked before, it will work again. As my personal sales coach Chuck Bauer says, "Don't overthink the think. Overdo the do!"

Well said, Chuck.

PART 3

WHAT?

CHAPTER  9

PLOT TWIST

Now that we have identified *who* our customers are and *where* to find them, *what* are we going to do about it?

Pop quiz. When someone asks you what you do for a living, what is your answer? For years I always said, "I'm in the insurance business." Here's the problem with that answer. The second I say "insurance," it immediately conjures whatever image they associate with my business. Believe it or not, many people have had a negative experience with insurance. Many more think insurance is a complete racket. They cringe every time they have to pay their premiums.

I changed my *what* several years ago when I started focusing on building a niche clientele. So now, when asked what I do, I answer with a more specific answer: "I insure companies that build, service, or maintain cell towers."

Most of the time I get the standard, "Oh, okay." But sometimes it creates a conversation that actually leads to a referral for a new client. One of the largest clients I ever landed came as a result of a what-do-you-do conversation.

So, *what* do you do? Now that you have had time to think about it, why not change up your standard answer? I'm not advocating you create an elevator pitch. I don't know about you, but I have never had a conversation of any kind while riding one. I just look at my phone and hope my fellow riders practice personal hygiene. But here is why I think it's important that you challenge your standard *what*.

Your *what* separates you from everyone else who works in the same *what*. Once I started telling people what I specifically insured, it changed the conversation. Something else it has done is remind me I am a specialist. I don't want to insure anything and everything. I have a specific target market I pursue. By stating that, it eliminates responses like, "Hey, my uncle owns a pawn shop. Can you insure him?"

Having a defined *what* will enable you to better serve your *who*—and reduce the chances that you receive the dreaded it's-over phone call, like I did.

When I look back on what caused me to lose that amount of business, I have to face the reality that we were no longer delivering the *what* our customers had grown accustomed to receiving. When you are starting out, your deliverables can vary as much as your customer base. The first few years of my career, my customer base included everything from manufacturing companies to dry cleaners—basically, anything and anyone who would let me insure them.

There was no rhyme or reason to anything I did. One day I was dealing with a restaurant, the next a contractor. I was a general practitioner, a mile wide and an inch deep, and the *what* I delivered was lackluster at best. For some clients, I was able to deliver a consistent product. For others, I just hoped and prayed my personality would keep their business.

News flash: hope is not a plan.

The sooner you clearly define your unique deliverable—your *what*—the sooner you will be able to improve your customer care and client retention.

CHAPTER  10

COMPARISON TRAP

Several years ago, I attended a talk given by Ellen Raulerson, a customer service expert. Among her many great points, one principle she shared rocked my world.

"Your customers aren't comparing you solely against your industry competitors," she said. "They compare you against *everyone* they buy a product or service from."

Read that again. Until that point, all I cared about was setting my service apart from other insurance agents. I figured so long as I was better than them, that's all that mattered. It wasn't.

My customers (and yours) buy a multitude of products and services. Every interaction with a salesperson or service provider is catalogued in their minds. As I type this from my satellite office

(Smitty's Cigar Lounge), I just overheard a conversation between the manager and their local cable provider. They were told a technician would come by in the next two to five hours. Two to five hours? How pathetic is that?! Unfortunately, we as consumers have been conditioned to accept such outrageous examples of customer nonservice—which is the very reason this book is needed.

Your *what* is the cafeteria of products and services you provide—and hopefully, it's better than the cable guy's. Of your *what*, can you clarify how it's uniquely better than what your customer currently has?

If you are struggling with answering that question, rest easy. I did too. My business is one of the most commoditized products in existence. In the insurance biz, we have to fight against a slew of common misconceptions. Take this one for example: "Give us fifteen minutes and we'll save you 15 percent!"

First of all, why would anyone do business with a gecko? Secondly, don't you want someone who's willing to spend more than a measly fifteen minutes on your insurance? My response to this slogan: if you want a computer to handle your coverage, then by all means, call their 800 number. The *what* that sets my business apart from theirs is time and quality of service.

I encouraged you in the first section to ask some tough questions about your *who*. You need to repeat that when it comes to getting real about your *what*. Put on your scuba gear and do a deep dive. Don't just accept the first answer. Keep asking yourself, "What is it that we do that serves our customers better than anyone else?"

This may take a while. That's okay. It's worth it!

One of the many benefits of writing a book is that it causes the author to reconsider whether they practice what they preach. I made a commitment long ago to never write or speak about principles I don't practice myself. Defining my *what* was a humbling experience. I had to admit my customers consistently bought from me for one of five reasons—and not one of them had anything to do with my great intellect!

What helped me define my *what* was simply going through my customer list and answering the following two questions: why did they initially buy from me, and why do they continue to buy from me?

When I did this, it uncovered five categories:

1. Compensation

We won one of our largest clients simply by agreeing to bring them on with reduced agent fees. They were being charged a boatload by a competing broker. When we asked them if they could quantify what they were getting in return for the price, they couldn't answer us. So, we presented them with a deliverable for less, and they agreed to hire us.

Over a ten-year period, their account grew ten times, and so did our compensation. It was a pure investment play on our part. We knew our day-to-day servicing and relationship skills would keep their business, but first we had to win it. On occasion, you may have to work for less in order to win an account. My experience is that you will make up for any losses over the long haul.

2. Coverage

I'm in the insurance business, so this category will need to be personalized to your industry. This would lean toward the technical aspect of your product offering. We have won business by uncovering deficiencies in their current coverage plan. This is another area where it pays to be a niche player. In five minutes, I can look at prospective clients' policies and know whether they are properly covered.

As I mentioned, we spend a lot more than fifteen minutes on our clients' insurance. In fact, this is where our coverage audit comes into play. We hired an insurance professor to help us with this. He does a complete audit of their existing coverage, and we come back to the client with our findings.

Regardless of your industry, finding deficiencies in their current product or service can help you win new business.

3. Claims

Most of the clients I have won in this category are a direct result of a competitor dropping the ball on a claims scenario. Go to your product or service. Ask this question: what is it supposed to do for the customer? When a competing product or service doesn't meet that need, that's when you pounce like a fat kid on a cupcake. Keep your eyes and ears open for customers who are disillusioned with their current supplier and make the call. There will never be a more opportune time to attack.

4. Compliance

We have won numerous clients by shoring up their program to meet and exceed industry requirements. Again, this may not be applicable to your product or service, or then again, maybe it is. When you know what's required and have a solution, you aren't seen as a vendor or peddler—you are a solution provider.

5. Contracts

This category primarily helps us retain customers. While it does play into winning new accounts, it has helped us in client retention more than anything else. Most of my clients are small to midsized companies. Most are under five hundred employees and don't have in-house counsel. Many have signed contracts in the past without realizing the potential pitfalls or additional risk they signed up for.

This is where our contract review comes in. We keep a contract specialist on retainer to review our clients' existing contracts. Then, we come back with a report that translates the legalese and explains the risks and liability they have assumed by entering into the contract. Contract reviews have proven to be a very big part of our value add.

Those are my *whats*. Sexy? Uh, no. Effective? Very. Your *what* doesn't have to be original or revolutionary to be powerful. You just have to deliver it in a powerful way.

A well-defined, concise, and clear *what* will take your customer care and client retention to a much higher level. Without it, you run the risk of being replaced by someone who *can* articulate it. Don't forget: your top client is someone else's top prospect!

CHAPTER 11

TRUTH SERUM

Finding your *what* can be as frustrating as trying to find Waldo. What we perceive as value may not ring true with who really matters—our customers.

As the old saying goes, "To a hammer, everything looks like a nail." When we win a client, we often assume it was our winning personality or product knowledge that sealed the deal. In reality, it was the timing of the purchase that swung it our way. We spent hours perfecting our presentation, but during our proposal meeting, the prospective client immediately turned to the last page to look at our pricing. They bought—and if I'm honest, we were a little disappointed that we weren't able to dazzle them with our charts and pie graphs.

A longtime client told me during our first meeting that if I ever walk into his office with a pie chart of any kind, that would be the last meeting I have with them. So now, when I bring them a pie, it's typically lemon meringue. For that client, I know what my *what* is. Actually, it happens to be a *who*. It's Tricia, who has serviced their account for almost twenty years now. Her level of daily attention keeps them as a client. On his best day, Bill Gates couldn't create a PowerPoint to compete with that.

A tip for honing in on your unique deliverable is to think through your typical day. What parts of it do you enjoy and thrive in? On the flip side, what about your day do you dread? Similar to the buffet illustration in chapter three, the same can be said of our attraction to and repulsion from daily tasks. We will complete the parts of our job that we truly enjoy at a much higher level than those that cause us to shudder.

Before I go any further, let me clue you in to something: you can't fake this. If you genuinely dislike a task, you will never be any good at it. You can put on a brave face and slog your way through it, but the end result will be a product that is subpar at best. Your customers deserve better than that—and they will get it. If not from you, then from your competitor.

Years ago, I had a well-meaning partner who tried his best to convince me I needed to ingrain myself more deeply in the technical aspects of our business. He encouraged me to conduct an exhaustive audit of my customers' policies, comparing the renewal coverage forms against expiring policies. I pored over the fine print of the policies, finding coverage gaps and deficiencies. For a minute, I felt really good about myself. I felt professional, like I was truly providing a value to my customer. That feeling was short-lived. I soon realized that while I was holed up in my office reviewing files like an accountant on April 14, my new sales efforts and relationship-building activities had suffered. I had to find a better way.

I did. I discovered that so long as that task was completed, it didn't matter who did the completing. Now my policy audits are conducted by an insurance professor. Literally. I keep him on retainer to review my client files. He has forgotten more about insurance coverage than I will ever know—and he loves it!

On a scale of one to ten, I would rank myself as a two at the technical side of my business. If I try really hard, attend every class available, and study my keister off, the best I can hope to get is twice as good as I am now. That makes me a four! My clients don't deserve a four. So, why wouldn't I team up with a ten?

Think of it this way: if the goal is climbing trees, would you rather hire a squirrel or train a horse?

Your customer doesn't care who provided the *what*. They simply want it done—and done better than anyone else. As you continue to further define your *what*, you may need to shift your thinking from ME to WE. What can your team provide your customers that sets you apart?

As of this writing, Aaron Rodgers is the highest-paid quarterback in the NFL. His job is to deliver the football to his teammates. He gets them the ball, they score the touchdowns. So, quit trying to score all by yourself. Hand the ball off or pass it to the open receiver. All that matters is winning.

CHAPTER 12

PROMISES, PROMISES

Sitting in Atlanta traffic, I looked ahead at the truck whose exhaust I was inhaling. Written across the back of it was their company slogan: "We keep all of our promises. Then again, we don't promise very much!"

How refreshing is that?

When asked about our service capabilities, many times do we feel it necessary to spout off everything we have ever done or thought about doing? This is dangerous. For many reasons, not the least of which is this: what if our customer believes us?

A former colleague of mine was infamous for bragging about how he had been a consultant for Fortune 500 companies. He actually put it on his résumé. Upon further review, his definition of consulting was a little broad. All we could ever corroborate was that yes, he had consulted with a Fortune 500 company. That company was Walmart. His "consulting" consisted of asking them the location of the nearest men's room! And we wonder why salespeople have to earn trust.

When it comes to defining and delivering our what, less is more. One promise kept is more powerful than one hundred promises made. It's similar to a corporate mission statement. If you can't recite it on demand, it isn't a good one. That's why my consulting company has a simple, one-sentence mission statement: "Guiding others to a life of success and significance."

Lofty? Yes. Doable? Abso-damn-lutely! I chose the term "guiding" because I want to be a tour guide instead of a travel agent. A travel agent tells you about various places to go and see, whether or not they have ever been there. A guide goes with you. They have been where you are going. They know the terrain. They have a vested interest in your experience.

By now, hopefully you have drilled down on your

deliverables. Maybe it's five things you do better than the competition, maybe it's one. The number is irrelevant. All that matters is your unwavering commitment that—no matter what—your customer will receive those things. Every single time.

Lastly, don't get hung up on how creative or cutting-edge your deliverables are. You don't have to be Elon Musk to be successful. At last count, Jeff Bezos, founder of Amazon, could write a personal check for every Tesla ever made. But there is nothing revolutionary about what Amazon does. Their what has been around for years. What is revolutionary about Amazon is how they deliver their *what*.

Strap in. We're going deep *how*-fishing.

PART 4

HOW?

CHAPTER  13

Secret Sauce

Answering the first three questions—*who*, *where*, and *what*—positions you to provide the service that will take your client care to a higher level. The answers to the next two questions—*how* and *when*—create the framework to provide your clients with an entirely new experience.

Your customer bought from you for a variety of reasons. Perhaps your product or service met an immediate need, and you were able to swoop in and save the day. Maybe you came out on top after a grueling RFP process. Regardless, it's vital to remember that what got them won't keep them.

Keeping clients depends solely on executing our how and when.

Although your *what* doesn't need to be unique (think Amazon), your *how* does. Somewhere along the line, Bezos and company committed to a customer experience (their *how*) unlike any other. Enter Amazon Prime. They didn't expand their product offering—they simply changed the manner in which it would be delivered. Free.

Not sure about you, but I LOVE free. Actually, I do know you—you love free as much as I do. Hence the reason we get an Amazon delivery nearly every day . . . and you probably do as well. With the increased amount of shipments, I have noticed a lot fewer disgruntled postal workers.

One of the best *hows* I have experienced came from an unlikely source: a server, whom we'll call Lou, at a high-end restaurant in Austin, Texas. When I travel to a new city, I rely on TripAdvisor to determine my dining choices. As of this writing, this restaurant is ranked number one of the 3,312 restaurants in Austin. That was enough for me to give it a shot.

Upon entering, it was like most fine-dining establishments, with a cheery hostess, a bustling bar scene, and an open kitchen so you can actually watch the chefs prepare your meal. They serve prime beef and fresh seafood, sourced from the finest fisheries in North America (their *what*). It's nice and all, but I've been there and done that.

What separated this restaurant for me was Lou. After we were seated, he came up, introduced himself, and—already knowing my name (the hostess told him)—he asked for my partner's name, John. Throughout dinner, he referred to us by name and made sure we were taken care of. It was at the end of dinner that Lou proved himself to be the top of all servers I've had the privilege of being served by. After settling up the bill (a big one, I might add), he asked us if they had met and exceeded our expectations. It did. He then did something I have never seen before at a restaurant. He handed us his business card. *His* business card. A server at a restaurant with a business card?

His request was simple. "Gentlemen, if you ever visit our fine city and restaurant again, I hope you will ask to sit in my section. I would love to make your next visit as fine as this one was."

I would say that's a pretty powerful *how*, wouldn't you? And I can promise you, the next time I travel to Austin, there is only one restaurant and one server I will dine with. Thank you, Lou—you are the man!

Take off your tie, kick off your shoes, lean your chair back, and let's come up with some wow-worthy *hows*. Deal?

CHAPTER 14

STAFF INFECTION

"You never get a second chance to make a first impression." There's a reason you've heard that saying for years—because it's true!

Here's a quick exercise for you. Call your office from a number your receptionist or first line of customer service won't recognize. How does it feel? Do you have to press one for English? Is your call "important to us and will be answered in the order it was received"? Are you placed on hold so long you actually hear more than one song? Ouch.

Now imagine a prospective customer is calling. You have spent days, months, maybe even years trying to win their business. Now you finally have your shot. They call you back and are greeted with, "Can I tell them what this is in reference to?" What a great way to make your prospective customer feel welcomed.

If your staff answers the phone with any of the above, you have a huge problem. That's because—take out your highlighter for this one—how you do anything is how you do EVERYTHING.

Read that again. And again.

If your team takes that tone with a big prospect, what will their response be when your existing customer calls with a problem? You might as well have them take a number and sit in a waiting room. Two places have those—the DMV and the doctor's office. Do you really want to be lumped in with those?

The uncomfortable truth is that you are communicating to your customer and potential customer the following:

1. You are hard to reach.

2. You don't trust their intentions (e.g. "Can I tell them what this is in reference to?").

3. They aren't important enough for you to know their name.

Compare this to the approach my mechanic takes. I have a fleet of six cars, which means I call often. And when I do, they answer the phone with a cheery,

"Jason, what can I do for you today?" I can actually tell they are smiling on the other end of the phone! Did I mention they are mechanics? Oh, and English is their second language. And yet, they know it's me calling and they call me by name. It's not just the owners—I expect them to care. It's the guy at the front desk and the guys in the service bays, too.

I have spent a fortune with them and have sent them countless referrals over the years. Their *what* is really simple. They repair my cars. Any mechanic can do that. It's their *how* that keeps me coming back.

Your customers expect the same from everyone in your company. Nobody gets a hall pass on this—nobody.

I recently had a bad experience with an airline. I found a deal on some tickets (their *what*) and, against my better judgment, I booked with them. I never fly with that airline, since Delta, my hometown airline, has always done a great job. But it was a cheap ticket, so I figured it was worth a shot.

It wasn't.

I called their customer service attendant, and, much to my dismay, they neither serviced nor were attentive. The price was right, but the *how* was terrible! I asked very simple questions and was made to feel like I was interrupting their day. I won't fly with them again. Now, I can't speak to the quality of their aircraft, the quality of their pilots, or their flight attendants. They may be as good or even better than Delta. What I can tell you is that they had the chance to be a hero for me—and missed it. A simple request was denied, and in so doing, they will miss out on future business.

Here's the thing. I fly a lot. My family loves to travel, and my travel bucket list is pretty impressive. Over a couple hundred dollars, one person ended up costing their company a ton of potential money. I'm not saying I would have left Delta, but what I am saying is that there is zero chance I will fly with them again.

Harsh? Maybe. But it's my money! I have a choice of who to spend it with. So does your customer. In my business, there is an insurance agent on every street corner—sometimes several. The manner in which my team and I respond to our customers every time we interact will determine whether they spend their money with us.

It's simple, but it's not easy, so let's talk about how to *how*.

CHAPTER  15

Survey Says

Before we dive in to methods and techniques on *how* to improve our how, I want to spend a minute on something I know *doesn't* work: customer surveys.

Now, if you are in the survey business, don't put the book down. I will admit my experience with surveys is limited. In a minute you will see why.

Late in 2014, my inbox was filled up by our corporate survey provider. Our company had hired a third-party consulting firm to compile customer feedback on a few key metrics, then report back to our individual salespeople and management. As the results came pouring in, I paid extra attention to the comments from our key clients. One particular client gave us all fives—the highest score—on every category. My chest swelled with pride.

Yep, I thought, *we are THAT good*.

Fast-forward a few weeks. That same customer—the one who gave us all fives—fired us.

What?! How could this be? They had just rated us as having great service and, more importantly, didn't list a single thing we could do to improve. Why would they do that?

The answer: they lied! It was easier and less confrontational than giving us the report card we actually deserved. Man, I wish my teachers would have taken that approach! They chose to rush through the survey, answering with what they thought we wanted to see. They basically gave us the "No, I'm just looking" response I give to shop attendants at the mall. It's a conditioned response—zero thought goes into it, and you get zero value from it.

Instead of peppering your customers with uncomfortable questions, most of which won't get an honest answer, remember the old saying—it's the quiet ones you gotta watch.

I didn't need a survey to tell me my relationship with that customer wasn't what it once was. The unreturned calls to his cell phone could—and should—have told me that. Instead, I rationalized it with excuses. "He's just busy! He knows how I feel about them."

He didn't. And soon, I would know how he really felt about us with two words: "You're fired!"

CHAPTER  16

EXTRA CREDIT

I grew up in a pastor's home. We went to church every time the door was open—Sunday morning, Sunday night, Wednesday night—every time. While I'm embarrassed to admit I don't remember all of the Bible stories and sermons I heard growing up, one particular story stands out. It captures the essence of *how*. It's the story of Rebecca, told in Genesis 24. It's worth a read, regardless of your religious persuasion.

I will provide an abbreviated version for you. Abraham (CEO) sends his top guy (senior vice president of sales) to find his son Isaac (junior partner) a wife. Top guy brings an entire entourage on the trip with him, along with ten camels. Upon arrival at their destination, they begin to set up camp when a beautiful young woman walks by. She's carrying water from the well for her family.

After a long journey, the top guy and his team are parched. He asks the woman for some water.

Her response is worlds more than he expected. Not only does the woman bring water for him, she offers to fetch water for his camels—all ten of them. Have you seen a camel lately? They are huge! And they drink a ton of water. How much, you ask? Up to twenty gallons at a time. I didn't go to MIT, but I can tell you watering ten camels takes a lot of work. Rebecca did what was asked of her *and then some*.

Fast-forward. Top guy picks her for Isaac. They marry and live happily ever after.

Moral of the story? Do what's expected—and then some. It's the "and then some" that separates the best from the rest.

What is your "and then some"?

Here's a hint: it's your *how*.

CHAPTER 17

FRESH INGREDIENTS

Now that I am firmly in my midforties and dangerously close to my late forties, I have noticed that my television-viewing habits have changed. While I used to channel-surf between sporting events, I now split time between my two favorite channels: Food Network and The Weather Channel. The reason I watch The Weather Channel is twofold: to make sure Jim Cantore is still alive (man, I hope he gets hazard pay) and to see if the forecast will be conducive to my hobby of outdoor cooking.

I look for every opportunity to spend quality time with my Big Green Egg. I absolutely love grilling and smoking meat. Steak, chicken, ribs, brisket, fish, pork shoulder, pizza, and macaroni and cheese. Yep, I smoke mac and cheese! My family says it tastes like eating a cigar covered in cheese, but I still love it! I guess it's an acquired taste.

When I started learning the ins and outs of all things meat, I figured why not learn from the best? Hence, Food Network. Bobby Flay, Guy Fieri, and Myron Mixon have become my new mentors. One thing I have noticed about these world-class chefs is that, while they all have a flair for the dramatic, they also focus on creating a repeatable process. As accomplished as they are, they still use a recipe. They have an end result they are looking for, and they know that if they use certain ingredients and seasoning on specific types of meat at a predetermined temperature and time, it will produce the same results—every time.

For customer care and client retention, the recipe looks something like this:

What + *How* = Experience

Experience + Time = Customer Satisfaction and Loyalty

Customer Satisfaction and Loyalty = Your Career

If you take meat (your *what*) and skimp on the grade of beef (your *how*), the end result will be a steak that can be good, but not great. Even Bobby pays the extra for prime. The moral of the story is you get what you pay for.

To create wow *hows*, you have to open your mind—and your wallet. You don't have to break the bank, but once in a while it wouldn't hurt.

One of my favorite examples of a wow how hangs prominently in my bar. A few years ago, I received a call from one of my key trading partners, Craig Lagos. I have done business with Craig for going on twenty years now. His what is providing my clients a customized payroll and HR-service platform. He is the VP of sales for People HR, a professional employer organization (PEO). While I have a multitude of PEOs at my disposal, there is only one Craig-o. He called one day to tell me he had something he wanted to drop by and give me at my office. He walked in with this:

See what it says? J. Peacock. I thought he had it made just for me.

"J-Bird," he said, "my wife and I saw it in an antique shop and HAD to get it for you!"

Craig could have easily called me and said, "Hey, I saw something you need. It's at an antique store, you should get it." I would have thanked him for thinking about me, because after all, it's the thought that counts, right? Only thing is, I can't hang his thought in my bar!

Do I even need to tell you who gets *all* my PEO business?

CHAPTER 18

RED CARPET

A few years ago, I had the responsibility of planning our annual Southeast regional sales meeting. Being in the Atlanta area, I had numerous options to consider. At the onset of planning, a few key factors came into play. I needed a location that was fairly close to the Atlanta airport, a venue that offered golf, and, most importantly, a location our CEO would approve of, since he would be writing the check.

Seeing as though I met him for the first time at a Ritz-Carlton, my gut told me I couldn't go wrong with hosting at one of their properties. My gut was right. It usually is. As big as it is and as much money as I have spent building it, I should listen to it more often!

From the very first planning call, I could tell

I would be in good hands. My event planner, Ashley, was extremely professional and patient. She walked me through every phase of the process. She asked questions—and listened. She didn't assume anything. Every detail was laid out in an easy-to-read format. She stayed away from using industry jargon and spoke with me in terms I could understand. As great as all of that was, that's not what made the experience memorable.

We were about a month out from the meeting when my grandmother passed away. After attending her funeral, I returned home and, like most people, was greeted with a stack of mail. As I leafed through the bills, magazines, and junk, one item stood out. It was a handwritten envelope with the Ritz-Carlton as the return address. I opened it to find a beautiful condolence card from Ashley. She wrote a nice note expressing her condolences and simply told me to call her when convenient. It was a Hallmark card. A card that she bought. A card with her handwriting in it.

To say I was blown away is an understatement. I have told that story to groups all over the United States, and it still amazes me. So simple, yet so powerful! Guess where our subsequent meetings were held?

The Ritz has a saying about their customer-service philosophy: "We are ladies and gentlemen, serving ladies and gentlemen." Compare that to another popular hotel slogan: "We'll leave the light on for you." What if I don't want the light on?!

I also need to mention that upon checking in to my room, I was greeted with a gift basket containing various treats from local suppliers. There were fresh peaches, a bag of peanuts, and a bottle of wine from a Georgia vineyard. I would have been impressed with all three items regardless of where they were purchased, but it was that extra thought of providing locally sourced gifts that really provided the wow factor.

Her *how* was treating me like a VIP. I appreciated it greatly. I still do.

So, go back to your product and service. How can you deliver a VIP experience? Better figure it out, because news flash: in your customer's eyes, they *are* a VIP.

CHAPTER

LEFT-HANDED LAY-UPS

Bear with me for a minute while I brag on myself. It won't take long.

Back in 1985, I was somewhat of a basketball star. With the hairstyle of Michael J. Fox, the shorts of Larry Bird, and the dribbling acumen of Magic Johnson, I was a force to be reckoned with. I had already accumulated my ten thousand hours on the basketball court, and it showed. But my eighth-grade coach, Kyle Detmers, saw that while I was the best player on the team, I was underachieving and depending too much on my athleticism.

One day after practice, he challenged me.

"Jason, anyone can make a normal lay-up. The real question is, can you make a left-handed lay-up?"

I really didn't understand what he was talking about.

"As you face better competition, they will force you to use your left hand by shutting off the right side of the lane," he explained. He had me bring the ball down the court, and as I typically did, I sprinted toward the right side of the lane. He immediately cut me off and made me go to my left. I was in trouble. My left-handed dribbling skills were lacking. He quickly stole the ball from me and said, "See what I mean?"

Embarrassed and frustrated, I went to work on learning how to play left-handed. Day after day, hour after hour, I honed my skills. Soon, I was able to dribble the ball with either hand and shoot right- or left-handed, depending on what side of the court I was on. It was a game changer—literally.

The same can be said of customer service. When you stay in the comfort zone of playing right-handed, you'll find yourself in trouble once you face tough competition.

Pairing your *what* with a powerful *how* will take your customer care and client retention to a higher level, regardless of the talent and tenacity of your competitors.

This next section pains me to write, but it illustrates the point above. Coach Nick Saban of the University of Alabama is simply the best in the business. Just typing that stings a little—okay, a lot. As a Georgia Bulldogs fan, it's a reminder of our painful losses against him, but I've got to hand it to him. Coach Saban is relentless when it comes to executing the details of his game plan. It's reported that he scheduled a meeting with his staff to discuss where to place the sign-up table at his summer football camp. After hours of discussion, the decision was made. When asked why he would take such painstaking measures for something so seemingly insignificant, he explained that since summer camp would be held every year, he wanted to decide once and for all where the table should be so they wouldn't have to revisit the decision again.

A table?! Yep. That's how detailed he gets. He is the living embodiment of the belief that how you do anything is how you do everything.

Why not take your service to a whole new level? Do what's expected, then add to it. Make it sizzle.

I will never forget my fortieth birthday. I celebrated it with some of my best insurance buddies at a world-class country club in South Carolina called Sage Valley. From the moment you enter the gates, you are treated like royalty. At Sage, I am Mr. Peacock.

After a round of golf, we were treated to a dinner fit for a king. From the bone-in rib eye to wine older than me, this meal was an occasion I will never forget. But what stole the show was a simple gesture that was executed to perfection. As dinner wrapped up, the entire kitchen staff approached our table singing "Happy Birthday." Atop a beautiful cake were forty lit candles. They baked me a cake—*me*!

I was and am still blown away by the class and thoughtfulness of that cake. It didn't happen by accident. My hosts from Summit Consulting made sure the staff knew it was my birthday and asked that they make it extra special. Mission accomplished. Mike, Fran, Pete, and John—you will never know how much that meant to me.

I know, it was just a birthday. But it's *my* birthday. It's important to me. My friends at Summit understand and live the principle of making what is important to that person just as important to you, as that person *is* to you.

What can you do to make what is important to your customer important to you? The answer to that question will help perfect your *how*.

PART 5
WHEN?

CHAPTER 20

STOP, DROP, AND ROLL

This next question will do more to help you keep the customers you want than any other I have discussed thus far. It will also position you to earn their introductions into new clients as well. The question at hand is *when*?

More specifically, *when* will you follow up and, more importantly, follow through on the commitments and promises you made to your customer? The correct answer to that is the ancient answer to most insurance questions—it depends.

It depends on what that customer needs. If it's an emergency, the *when* needs to be NOW. Here's the thing about client emergencies. You and I both know that what your client perceives as an emergency is oftentimes not an actual emergency. But—and it's a big but—if they think it is, then it is.

Your response time for these situations has to be quick and, more importantly, consistent. Believe me, I am all for establishing boundaries, and as I have alluded to in prior chapters, I have had some clients take advantage of those. Thankfully, most of my clients don't. There are even a few whom I rarely hear from. When I do, I know it's an emergency. When this happens, we go into a mode made famous by one of my former partners, Bruce Eades: Mega 911!

The above should go without saying, but in this day and age of "press one for English," getting an immediate response to a pressing issue can be difficult. You may not be able to immediately solve the crisis, but you need to at least respond with the effort to do so.

I'm not saying you need to be the point person for all client emergencies. In fact, I suggest that you not be. And that sets up the perfect segue into the next principle of keeping your clients.

CHAPTER  21

CAST OF CHARACTERS

I love the theater. By the way, I just typed that using a British accent. Not sure why I insist on pronouncing "theater" like that. And now, you just pronounced it like that too.

Everything about theater—the music, the dancing, the costumes, the overacting—is fantastic! Part of my love of theater stems from watching my daughters, Cameron and Kylee, perform in their high-school musical theater program. Thankfully, they got their looks from their mother, but they got their stage talents from me!

One thing every show or play has in common is a playbill. If you aren't hip to the theater scene, a playbill is basically an outline of the play or musical. It lists the scenes in chronological order, along with the cast of characters in order of appearance. The playbill prepares the audience for *what* is about to happen, along with *when* it will happen, and, most importantly, *who* will be involved.

You need to do the same when it comes to preparing your customer for the next act. As part of your new customer onboarding process, I recommend you provide them with your cast of characters. Who in your company will be working with them? If it's just you, then I suggest you look into hiring a virtual assistant. Even the Lone Ranger had Tonto.

As you introduce your team, it's vital that you educate the customer on your teammates' roles. Just like the playbill, you need to set expectations. As discussed in the previous chapter, some customer issues will need to be handled by whoever is available at the time of the emergency. Don't get caught up in departments or titles during a Mega-911 scenario. As the late Ross Perot said, "If you see a snake, just kill it—don't appoint a committee on snakes."

Your *when* is also a crucial part of setting client expectations. When it comes to determining the timeline for your service, you need buy-in from the folks who will actually be providing it. A surefire way to get in hot water with your team is to commit them to a when that is unrealistic. Creating a realistic service timeline is absolutely necessary so you don't overpromise and underdeliver.

But a timeline won't happen overnight—you and your team will have to go through your list of typical *whats* and measure them with a response rate. While there will be some unique scenarios, most service deliverables are performed repeatedly. What's great about repeated tasks is that you can establish standard operating procedures (SOPs). With SOPs in place, you can commit yourself and your team to delivering your *what* within a consistent *when*.

I must warn you—be careful when committing to delivery timelines. Inconsistent delivery is a recipe for disaster. I have won many clients because of inconsistent delivery from *other* people. Their prior agent wined and dined them during the courting process, but once the invoice was paid, the agent went missing. Phone calls went unreturned, emails unread, deliveries undelivered. To prevent this from happening to our customers, we commit to only a handful of deliverables during a contract year. Then we deliver them every time, on time.

An example of a powerful *when* is Jimmy John's.

They have become famous not so much for the quality or uniqueness of their *what* (sandwiches), but for their industry-leading *when* (delivery). Their average delivery time (between five and twenty minutes) is so short they actually coined the phrase "Freaky Fast." One of the ways they accomplish this *when* is by limiting the radius of delivery. This one decision enables them to consistently live up to their reputation of being "Freaky Fast."

I mentioned that my airline of choice is Delta. Over the past few years, they have focused on one of their *whens*: baggage handling. They have created an SOP that results in a twenty-minute delivery of your luggage to the baggage claim. In most cases, my bag is already waiting for me by the time I reach the carousel.

Neither Jimmy John's nor Delta arrived at their *when* commitments haphazardly. Reams of data and prior experience went into that commitment. You, too, must tread lightly while in the process of developing your *whens*. Once you arrive at a reasonable and repeatable *when* commitment, LIVE by it.

There is nothing worse than hearing, "But you said . . ." from an angry customer, so follow these tips and ensure your *when* leads to a *win*.

CHAPTER 22

BAD NEWS BEARERS

This *when* may be the most important *when*, and also the most difficult: when you have to deliver bad news.

I will never forget the call I received one afternoon from a key client of mine. She was the CFO of one of my largest accounts and had become a dear friend. When her name popped up on my caller ID, I actually got excited. She was that kind of a client, one you want your entire portfolio to resemble.

When I answered her call, I could tell something was wrong. Through tears and a faint voice, she gave me the news that one of their employees had fallen off of a cell tower. As you can imagine, the outlook was grim. The tower was 240 feet tall. Did I mention I am in the insurance business? More specifically, I provide workers' compensation coverage. This claim would not be pretty.

To make matters worse, I had bound the workers' comp coverage with a new insurance provider less than twenty-four hours before the accident. The relationship with this provider was brand new. They had done me a huge favor by agreeing to insure this company in the first place, and now I had the unenviable task of breaking the news that we were now looking at a claim that could cost them millions.

I sat on my back deck and thought of every possible way to soften the news. There wasn't one. A claim of this magnitude would send shock waves through any company, especially one we just started working with. With fear and trepidation, I called my guy at the insurance company. Let me repeat that—I *called* him. In this age of email, texts, Snapchat, Twitter, and every other medium of communication, I chose the one you need to choose when it comes to delivering bad news.

Pick up the phone and call!

You can't relay emotion through a keyboard. He

needed to hear it straight from the source—me. He needed to hear the awkward silence that followed when I broke the news to him. I didn't have an answer for why it happened. I didn't skirt the subject of how awful it was. It was real, and a life hung in the balance.

That was one of the hardest conversations I have ever had. As hard as it was, I'm thankful I did. I didn't hide behind an email or text. The final amount of the claim? It's still being paid. To date, it's well over seven million dollars. Miraculously, the guy lived and has received every conceivable type of medical treatment.

My relationship with the insurance company? Stronger than ever. They continue to be one of my go-to providers. Had I not handled the claim in that manner, our relationship very well could have been damaged or terminated.

So, when you are greeted with bad news—and you will be—take a deep breath and be the one your customer hears it from. Don't let them hear it from anyone else. It's your relationship. Own it!

CHAPTER 23

EXHIBIT A

On occasion, customers will test our last nerve. In moments like these, you will want to tell them several things, most of which end with either "you" or "off." This book is family friendly, so you can figure out what goes in front of those.

One such moment happened very early in my insurance career. I had been slinging policies for about three years when my wife informed me we were having baby number three. Actually, she had my son Tanner, who was all of three years old, tell me. A simple "Mommy has a baby in her tummy!" said it all. I was already under a mountain of pressure to increase my production, and now baby number three?!

Shortly after, I received a phone call that sent my stress level into the stratosphere. My largest client at the time decided to give our insurance program to a competing broker. This exercise is known in the insurance business as a broker of record change. Upon receiving this news, my initial response probably contained both "YOU" and "OFF!"

After regaining my composure, I went into damage-control mode. I called my partner in Savannah, who cobrokered the account with me, and got his account executive, Cathy, who handled the day-to-day service on the phone. She was in tears. She worked her tail off taking care of this client. To be treated like this was salt in the wound.

My partner, Danny, immediately booked a flight to Atlanta. We then went into Mega-911 mode. I asked Cathy how often she touched their account on a monthly basis.

"Monthly?" she said. "Jason, I touch their account every day, several times a day!"

That gave me an idea. I told her to print out their service logs—all of them. Since the inception of our relationship, every client touch and service entry had been logged in our system. It took reams of paper to print them all. Reams! Danny had to pack a separate bag just to bring them on the plane.

Armed with our data, we walked into the client's office. His greeting was less than friendly. He was sheepish and knew he had screwed us over. I could feel my blood pressure rise. He informed us yet again that he had decided to go with another broker and thanked us for our past service.

Although it's almost twenty years ago, I'm still proud of my response. Maybe it was youthful brashness, but I met his words with a response of my own. I reached into the bag of data, pulled out a stack of paper that would kill an elephant, and dropped it on his desk.

"I'm glad you mentioned our past service," I said. "This stack of paper covering your desk is proof of our service. Look at it! Now, I'm sure the guy you gave our business to is making promises on what he is going to do. Your desk is now covered with what we have done."

He rescinded the broker of record transaction and we walked out of his office, business in hand.

Sometimes your *when* is proof that you do what you say you will do. Moral of the story? Keep track of when and what you do for your clients. You may have to present them as Exhibit A in the court of customer keeping.

CHAPTER 24

SAVE THE DATE

While putting together your *when* plan, my advice is to pull out a calendar. Once your deliverables are determined, I encourage you to collaborate with your customer on when they will be delivered. This is where the calendar of services comes in.

I am a big proponent of simplicity. On the following page is a sample of what I use with my own clients.

During both new client onboarding and ongoing client servicing, the simple act of creating and, more importantly, committing to specific actions on specific dates will help prevent deliverables from falling through the cracks and set you up to win the *when*.

Another benefit from using a calendar of services

is that it provides one of the best opportunities to brag on your support staff. Go back to the example of mine. You see the column that reads "Person Responsible"? The more people on your team who can own a service deliverable, the better. It shows that the client is not just your client, but your whole team's client. Involving your team members will deepen the client relationship and provide you with the chance to give credit where it is due—to your team.

ANNUAL SERVICE PLAN
Jan 1, 2020 – December 31, 2020

Client: ABC Company

Commitments

- Policy Binding and Delivery
- Certificate of Insurance Holders Notified
- Subcontractor Agreement Review
- MSA Review
- Claims Analysis
- EMR Analysis and Forecast
- Mid-Year Review
- Renewal Data/Submission Sent

NEXT STEPS

Action Item / Person Responsible / Due Date

1.	Coverage Placed/Binders sent to ABC	TH	1/1/20
2.	All COI's emailed to holders	TH	1/1/20
3.	Sub agreement audit with rec's	JP/EB	4/1/20
4.	MSA Analysis with rec's	EB	4/1/20
5.	Loss Analysis/Trend report	NR	3/1/20
6.	Stat Card Report/EMR Forecast	KF	7/1/20
7.	6 month payroll/sales/ claims report	TH/JP	7/1/20
8.	Renewal Exposures Submitted to Market	TH	10/1/20

CHAPTER  25

WRAPPING UP

So, there you have it. The five questions: *who, where, what, how,* and *when*?

I trust that my answers to them have jostled loose some answers of your own. If you want to use my answers, that's fine too. I don't mind at all. In fact, it would be the first time in my life that my answers are the ones being used—I usually "borrowed" the answers of whoever was sitting next to me in class.

I want to leave you with two parting thoughts. One has to do with your career, the other with your life.

My final piece of advice regarding finding and keeping customers has to do with developing deep client relationships. To create long-term client relationships, you need multiple relationships within the client organization, and they need multiple relationships within yours. People within your client organizations come and go. If your relationship is solely with the outgoing person, guess what? Your relationship just left as well.

The more people you involve in the customer-keeping process, the better your odds of surviving a turnover of personnel. I have been on the losing end of having singular client relationships far too many times to mention. Word to the wise is, unless your client's name is on the building, they are subject to leave.

My advice: build relationships with the people whose names are on the building, on their office door, and on their shirt. Whether it's the CEO (building), management (office door), or rank and file (shirt), the more relationships you develop, the longer you will keep them.

Last but not least, let's talk about you. The final question for you is *why*?

Why do you do what you do? The business of sales and customer service can be grueling. It certainly has its ups and downs. When I'm asked if I ever thought about quitting, I answer, "Only twice—twice a day, every day!"

So, what keeps you going?

Only you can answer that. Don't apologize for your answer. If it's money, then by all means, make all you can. If it's prestige and promotions, awesome—go get that next promotion. If it's making your mark on the world and leaving behind a legacy, fantastic. Make that mark.

For me, it's the Fab Five.

That would be my wife, Wendy, and my three kids, Tanner, Cameron, and Kylee. They have been and always will be my *why*.

The picture on the following page has sat on my desk for over fifteen years. Whenever I didn't *feel* like picking up the phone and banging out cold calls, I looked at it. Whenever I dreaded responding to an upset customer, I looked at it. Whenever my commission check was less than stellar, I looked at it.

The people in that picture need me. I am responsible for them, to house, clothe, feed, and educate. I don't have the luxury of waiting for my phone to ring. I don't have a plan B. I don't have a rich uncle who will one day leave his fortune to me.

Here's the thing. The little ones in that picture grow up—fast. Time flies, my friend. Soak it up.

Thank you for sticking with me through this book. I hope it serves as a resource in your continual quest to find and keep the customers you want.

And remember: the road to success just might be your driveway.

ABOUT THE AUTHOR

 For over twenty-five years, Jason Peacock's career has centered around one thing: sales. Whether it was the streets of Chicago or corporate boardrooms, his career path has been paved by an ability to create and maintain customer relationships. As a top-performing insurance agent, founding partner, and agency manager, Jason has a unique perspective from being able to relate to those on the front lines of selling, as well as those involved with management and leadership. Through his books, speaking engagements, and live workshops, Jason's passion is "paying it forward" to the next generation of sales professionals.

Jason and his wife, Wendy, are the proud parents of their three adult children, Tanner, Cameron, and Kylee. They reside in Gainesville, Georgia.

FOLLOW
JASON PEACOCK

 JasonCPeacock.com

 Facebook.com/JasonPeacockInc

 @JasonPeacockInc